FOLLOWING GOD ONTO THE STAGE

A 40-Day Devotional Journey

Marked Writers
PUBLISHING

Alisa Hope Wagner

3 John 1.2

alisa hope wagner

D1291890

ISBN-13: 978-0692845431
ISBN-10: 0692845437
BISAC: Religion / Christian Life / Devotional

FOLLOWING GOD
ONTO THE STAGE

A 40-Day Devotional Journey

INTRODUCTION

I enjoy pushing myself physically because I've come to realize that stretching and growing in one area of my life will automatically help me to stretch and grow in other areas of my life. Not only have I grown physically stronger during my nine months of physical training, I've also grown mentally, emotionally and spiritually stronger. I want to claim God's promise that I can "prosper in all things." I desire for each detail of my life on earth to be submitted to the Lord, so He can prosper every aspect with His goodness, grace and mercy. My goal is to be fully mature in Christ when I leave this earth and enter into heaven for eternity.

"Beloved, I pray that you may prosper in all things and be in health, just as your soul prospers" (3 John 1.2 NKJV).

Competing in a bodybuilding competition is just one of many ways we can achieve victory by digging into the strength of God. There is no win without the struggle. There is no change without the fight. Many of us feel like our lives are stagnating because we haven't taken a risk in a while. That risk doesn't have to be physical. We can start a new adventure any time with the Lord's help. We simply need to ask Him which direction He is leading us, so He can establish our steps of victory.

"The heart of man plans his way, but the LORD establishes his steps" (Proverbs 16.9 ESV).

We can take a class, read a book, form a new habit, begin a new hobby, start a new venture, etc. The opportunities surrounding us are boundless, and we have the unlimited supply of God's strength to empower us. There is nothing we can't achieve if God wills it. When God gives us His *yes*, it's not about *if* we can; rather, it's about *how* we can. So try something new with the Lord today, and watch as your life expands and prospers in all areas!

"For no matter how many promises God has made, they are 'Yes' in Christ. And so through him the "Amen" is spoken by us to the glory of God" (2 Corinthians 1.20 NIV).

DEDICATION

God, my Creator, my Savior, my Counselor

Daniel, my high school sweetheart and soul mate

Isaac, my firstborn son

Levi, my brown-eyed boy

Karis Ruth, my cherished girl

Christina, my twin and friend

Church Unlimited, my church

Thank you to Faith Wilde for being my trainer extraordinaire and to my aunt, Patti Coughlin, for taking the time to edit the final draft of this devotional book.

DAY 1: THE SPRAY TAN

Spray tan is a bodybuilder's best friend and worst enemy. Since I was competing in the physique division, I had to get sprayed by the orange-brown paint three times. Two coats Friday evening and my third coat Saturday morning before the competition. I couldn't wear deodorant. I couldn't wear perfume. I couldn't take a shower for twenty-four hours. It's a fairly gross experience. The competitors actually have to bring black sheets and pillowcases to the hotel, so they don't get smudges of the tan tint all over the bed.

Under the bright lights of the stage, the dark tan looks amazing. It covers all kinds of blemishes, it makes the muscles more pronounced and it prevents lighter skin from looking washed out. In fact, the spray tan almost makes the competitor look perfect from a distance. I have freckled skin, but from the stage my skin looked flawless. However up front, the spray tan tells a different story. The dye actually made my freckles darker close up. And it made my faded stretch marks visible again. The tint also mixed with my sweat and made dirty-like blotches all over my body. I looked unnatural and distorted face-to-face. I didn't smell too good either.

I like to compare spray tan to the law. The law is the opposite of grace. The law is humankind's effort to try to be perfect before a holy God and before others. When we put the law above grace in our daily life, we might look perfect on stage from a distance, but up close the law actually magnifies our imperfections. Only grace can offer us a perfect holiness that we can't achieve on our own. When you look at the life of someone who clings onto grace, you may see their flaws, but they are beautiful under the glorious light of Jesus' grace.

"For sin shall no longer be your master, because you are not under the law, but under grace" (Romans 6.14 NIV).

God, I struggle with understanding law versus grace. But I do know that law magnifies my mistakes and grace erases them. I am saved by grace through Jesus Christ. I am the righteousness of God only through His work on the Cross. I don't want to fall into the trap of the law, trying to be good enough to please You or trying to be good enough to deserve a relationship with You. Help me to not hide my flaws. I don't need to look perfect in front of others. I trust that I can reveal my weaknesses, knowing that Your strength will be seen in them. I pray this in Jesus' name, amen.

Questions

- Do you try to be perfect in front of your family and friends?
- Do you have flaws or weaknesses that you wish to cover up?
- How can you claim your righteousness by faith?

You are saved by grace alone!

DAY 2: POSE OFF

My physique division was separated into two groups: Group A was under 5'4" and group B was over 5'4". Since I am 5'7", I was in Group B. I was excited to win first place in my group, but I had no idea about the events that would ensue because of that win. When I walked off stage relieved that my time in the spotlight was over, I had to set down my trophy and walk right back onto stage again. I had no idea what I was supposed to do when I got out there. Then the winner of Group A joined me, and we stood in front of hundreds of people including several intent looking judges. Suddenly, the announcer explained to the audience that we would be doing a pose off. I had never done a pose off before, but when the music started, I had no choice but to get moving.

Luckily, I had practiced my poses over and over again that they came naturally to me. Plus, I decided to throw a few poses in there that I hadn't practiced but had seen done just to fill up more time. I felt so nervous, but my family and friends said that I looked confident and calm while performing. My brain was in such a state of stage fright that I relied on body memory for the 60 seconds of the pose off. If I hadn't performed those poses for months before the competition, I'm sure my mind would have gone blank and I would have run off stage!

Jesus told His disciples to never worry about what they would say before others because the Holy Spirit would give them the right words. This doesn't necessarily mean that God will miraculously put His Words into our hearts; rather, it means that the Holy Spirit will pull from the treasure trove of words that we have stored up from our daily reading and prayer. God will arrange the words in perfect order to influence the audience that confronts us. During my pose off, I would have never been able to do the poses if I hadn't stored them in my mind and muscle memory. That same goes for our words. In order to be used as witnesses for God, we need to store His words in our heart everyday by listening to His Voice and reading His Word, the Bible. God will then access those words and choose the right ones for us to say at just the right time to have the best effect on those who are listening.

"When they drag you into their meeting places, or into police courts and before judges, don't worry about defending yourselves—what you'll say or how you'll say it. The right words will be there. The Holy Spirit will give you the right words when the time comes" (Luke 12:11-12 MSG).

God, help me to store up Your words in my heart everyday because I know that "...For the mouth speaks what the heart is full of" (Luke 6.45). I don't want my mind to go blank when people ask me relevant questions about You. Plus, I want to have a solid foundation of Your Word that even if I'm asked a question for which I don't have an answer, I can at least give an honest examination of it. I want my heart to be so filled with Your Voice and the Bible that even when I'm nervous, the Holy Spirit can take over and draw from Your wisdom that I've gathered over the years. I pray this in Jesus' name, amen.

Questions

- How often do you study God's Word?
- Has the Holy Spirit Spoken through you?
- Has God ever given you His words when you need them?

Store up God's Words!

DAY 3: GUILTY MORNINGS

Towards the end of training for my bodybuilding competition, I started to wake up with guilt each new day. The rigorous exercise schedule and strict diet leave no room for error, and life becomes a finite line of discipline and sacrifice. I felt guilty if I went over in one of my macros. I felt guilty if I stayed up too late. I felt guilty if I had too much coffee. I felt guilty if I didn't labor hard enough in one of my workouts. Every morning I would look at my previous day and analyze how I had failed to achieve the perfection that I had set for myself. No matter how hard I tried, I could not be completely flawless in every area.

I wanted to project perfection to others, but I knew if I did, I would be living a lie. I had a choice. I could be honest about my failings and accept grace or I could act like my training was seamless and I met the difficult standards each day without fail. I decided just to humble myself and let people know that training was hard and I struggled with keeping the strict parameters of my training. I was tired of feeling guilty each morning. God knows I'm not perfect and He loves me. No matter what, I was working hard and achieving goals that were once impossible for me. God understands that I'm not perfect, which is why He sent His Son, Jesus, to die for me. He wants to work in my weakness (2 Corinthians 12.9).

We may try to project perfection because we are worried about what others think. Or we may very well be our worst critic, feeling guilty if we can't meet our own impossible expectations. But if we do our best and focus on what God thinks, we can be released from a cycle of failure and guilt. We will never be perfect, but Jesus didn't come to this world to condemn us. He came to free us. Life is too short and we have too much to accomplish to be filled with guilt every morning.

Giving our all may never reach a 100% success rate, but Jesus' grace fills in the rough edges of our effort. Even in our weakness, we are strong. Even in our failure, we win. And in our imperfection, we are perfected through Christ.

"For by one sacrifice he has made perfect forever those who are being made holy" (Hebrews 10.14 NIV).

Father, I know I will never be perfect. Show me how I can be confident even in my failures because I'm tired of waking up with guilt each morning. I know that Jesus didn't come to this world to condemn me, but to free me from the constant judgment of others and myself (John 3.17). I may never be perfect, but I want to give you my all. I won't try to earn Your approval. I trust that I am already completely loved and accepted. But I do want to do my best to make You smile down on me. I love You, Father. In my joy of what You have done for me, I want to live my life to the fullest. I will stumble and fall, but I know that You are cheering me to get back up and run for You again. I pray this in Jesus' name, amen.

Questions

- Do you struggle with feelings of guilt?
- How does grace prevent projecting false perfection?
- What good things has God achieved in your weakness?

You are free from guilt!

DAY 4: SCRUTINIZING

Standing on stage in a competition suit is very humbling for me. It's a vulnerable experience having judges analyze every aspect of my physique. Nothing is missed. Every muscle, ounce of fat, bone and even vein is put under the microscope. The bright lights of the stage shine down, and I feel completely exposed. I am in essence presenting hours of training, sacrifice, energy and effort for others to scrutinize and grade. No matter how hard I have worked, the immense pressure of the stage can be exhausting and intimidating. Luckily, stage time goes quickly, and the feeling of relief and accomplishment take over once I make it backstage. I've seen the areas in which I need to improve, and I can apply that knowledge for my future training.

Many times God will shine a bright light on our lives, exposing all the details that are sometimes hidden. When He does this, we may feel like we are being scrutinized, but God is not condemning us. He is simply trying to get us to see areas that we may be ignoring, hiding or denying. Being vulnerable before God does not have to be scary. He is not judging us; rather, He is jealous for us to grow into the beautiful designs He has for us. And He will not keep us under the bright lights for long. Once the areas of improvement are exposed, He quickly pours His peace and comfort into the rawness. He loves us, and wants us to improve. He knows that we have this one life to become the people we will be for eternity.

Some people fear the revealing bright lights of God's pruning. They run away from His stage of refinement because they don't want to be vulnerable. But God is good, and He has our best interests at heart. He loves us too much to leave us in our comfortable mediocrity. He wants to mold us into the perfect image of Jesus. He is working that seed of salvation from the inside out (Philippians 2.12-13). Every time He exposes an area that is not His best for us, we are given the ability to apply the knowledge we have learned. God will not leave us on the stage for long, and we will feel good that we examined areas that we can make more *blessable* for God.

"Search me, O God, and know my heart; test me and know my anxious thoughts. Point out anything in me that offends you, and lead me along the path of everlasting life" (Psalm 139.23-24 NLT).

Father God, I want to be vulnerable on your refining stage, so You can mold me more into the image of Your Son. I know that I have grace for my flaws, but that doesn't mean that I shouldn't try to improve those areas. Help me to trust that You are not judging me. You are simply jealous for me to be more than I am now. Reveal to me with Your bright light of truth anything that may offend You, and help me to adjust my course along Your "path of everlasting life." I give You the raw material of my life, knowing that You will make me into something pleasing and beautiful. I pray this in Jesus' name, amen.

Questions

- Has God tried to shine His bright life of truth on you?
- Have you ever found yourself on stage with God?
- What area is God trying to expose in your life today?

Let God search your heart!

DAY 5: STACKED DAYS

I trained six months for my second bodybuilding competition. Towards the end, I was exercising two or three times a day. My diet had become extremely strict. My thoughts were consumed with the extreme lifestyle I was forging. Each work out began to blend with the next, and I could no longer see the light at the end of the tunnel. Each day, each work out, each bench press, each squat, each pull-up and each deadlift seemed to make no difference in my physique. I was too close and too thick into training that I couldn't see the changes my efforts were producing. But I knew from experience that changes aren't made over night. The biggest advances we make are made up of tiny steps, not giant leaps, along the way. I wound up doing well in my competition, and I'm glad I didn't let myself get distracted by the small picture.

King David may have beat Goliath in an instant, but he actually won the fight over years of practicing his slingshot in the wilderness as he watched his father's sheep. And God didn't give David Goliath right away. First, God had David fight the lion to protect his sheep. Next, God had David fight the bear to protect his sheep. Each one of those victories brought David closer to defeating Goliath and the Philistines, protecting God's Children. David could have gotten discouraged. He could have given up on developing his skill because he didn't see that Goliath was waiting just around the corner. Instead, David chose to trust God and make those tiny steps of improvement, trusting that they would eventually add up to one giant leap.

It is difficult when we are in the thick of our struggle to see the bigger picture. But we have to trust that if we are faithful everyday to the process, those days will stack up and help us to attain the victory.

Bodybuilding can be applied metaphorically to life. God has Goliaths in store for us, and we won't be ready to fight them if we squander the small steps every day that lead to our victory. Our "training" may never be perfect, but we can definitely remain committed. We don't have to get discouraged because we know that nothing comes back void (Isaiah 55.11). All our efforts combined will eventually produce something powerful and great that the Lord can use to change lives and establish His glory.

"David said to the Philistine, 'You come against me with sword and spear and javelin, but I come against you in the name of the LORD Almighty, the God of the armies of Israel, whom you have defied'" (1 Samuel 17.45 NIV).

Father, help me not to get distracted on this path that You have set before me. I trust that all of my steps of obedience will equal to something wonderful for Your glory. I want to keep my eyes on the bigger picture that You are establishing on earth. I want to be ready to attain the victory when my "Goliath" confronts me. Help me to be prepared as I stay faithful to the small steps of obedience along the way. But most of all, help me to rely on Your strength and Your promises. Only You can accomplish the great and mighty things You have in store for me. I pray this in Jesus' name, amen.

Questions

- What small steps are you making for a bigger cause?
- Is there a Goliath that God is preparing you to fight?
- How are your efforts going to pay off?

Keep your eyes on the bigger picture!

DAY 6: CROOKED

I didn't realize that my body was slightly crooked until I started lifting heavy weights. My hip and thoracic spine are both a little tilted to one side, and all my life I compensated. When I began squatting heavier weight, I leaned to one side, causing one quadriceps to grow slightly larger than the other. Also, both my shoulders are tight, and the range of motion—especially in my left arm—is limited. The imbalance in my body became increasing apparent, so I finally went to the chiropractor. He explained that everyone has a slight tilt to his or her body, but it goes unnoticed unless the body is put under great pressure. Lifting heavy weights allowed the unevenness in my body to finally present itself.

Once I became aware of my body's limitation, I was able to work with it better because I knew what to look for. During my squats, I focused on using both legs equally to lift the weight. I also began stretching my shoulders, so I could open them up and equalize their range of motion. Although my body will always be a little crooked, I am better prepared to modify my workouts to better cope with the imbalance. Hopefully, if I keep working on maintaining great form, I may be able to almost eliminate any sign of my crooked hip and spine.

The same goes for life. We may not know that we have imbalance in our life until we are put under great amounts of pressure. The weight of circumstances does an excellent job at revealing any unevenness in our beliefs, thoughts, actions and faith that we may have accepted as normal. Many times, God uses the pressures of the world to strengthen us and create more balance in our lives, but we have to be aware that the problem exists. When we finally see the problem areas, we can set our focus on making modifications to improve and

19

even eliminate any crookedness within our mind, heart, words, actions, relationships, etc.

"Dear brothers and sisters, when troubles of any kind come your way, consider it an opportunity for great joy. For you know that when your faith is tested, your endurance has a chance to grow. So let it grow, for when your endurance is fully developed, you will be perfect and complete, needing nothing" (James 1.2-4 NLT).

God, I know that the pressures of this world reveal the areas of my life that are not totally dependent on You. I thank You because I know these pressures are growing my faith and creating more balance in my Christian walk. Help me to see those crooked areas that need to be modified and refined. Also, help me not to become anxious or nervous when those weak spots of my life are revealed. I know it may take time, but You are strengthening me little by little. Teach me to rely on You. I can't carry this weight alone. I ask for Your strength and endurance to flood my life. I pray this in Jesus' name, amen.

Questions

- What recent pressures have exposed life imbalance?
- How can you compensate for revealed weaknesses?
- Has God intervened when you've buckled under pressure?

God will get you through it!

DAY 7: INJURIES

Minor injuries are a normal part of weightlifting. No matter if you lift weights with a trainer, lift weights with friends or lift weights solo, some part of your body will get damaged and will become inflamed for a few days or a few weeks. Once you get an injury, you must modify your workouts. It can be very frustrating not being able to fully use every muscle because of one muscle that is in distress, but you press through. Quitting over minor injuries is not an option, since the alternative would be muscle atrophy from disuse. The inflammation will finally fade, and the body will become stronger and better able to avoid the injury in the future.

I had a few such injuries during my training. I pulled my trapezius while doing pull-ups and I pulled my groin muscle while doing weighted leg lifts. No matter how well I watched my form, something happened to cause those muscles to become irritated. Since this was my second bodybuilding competition, I was accustomed to the setback. Instead of becoming upset, I just dealt with the problem, knowing that it would eventually heal. As long as I stretched, ate the right foods, drank plenty of water and incorporated other healing options (hot baths, cold packs, essential oils, chiropractor, massage, etc.), I knew that I would heal quickly. I wasn't going to quit because of a few minor hindrances.

Many people are surprised when they get hurt in relationships, but we all step on each other's toes once in a while. The alternative would be to get rid of relationships altogether, but that would go against Jesus' emphasis on loving one another (John 13.34) The Bible says we are like sandpaper to each other, which doesn't sound very pleasant, but it is for our good because it is refining us. Yes, it is true that some relationships are toxic and must be cut out completely for a time or indefinitely, but minor relational infractions are a normal part of life. No one is perfect, and we are just as flawed as the next person. And "it is to one's glory to overlook an offense" (Proverbs 19.11 NIV).

"As iron sharpens iron, so a friend sharpens a friend" (Proverbs 27.17 NLT).

Lord, help me not to become overwhelmed and frustrated because of minor relational infractions. I know that we all mess up, and I don't want to become offended by every little thing. I am strong in You, and people will never be perfect, especially me. I want to offer mercy freely, so I too can receive mercy freely. Show me how to incorporate healing methods into my life (prayer, Bible reading, Christian music, self-awareness, godly relationships, saying sorry, forgiving easily, etc.) that will help me to heal quickly from the minor injuries that I receive on a daily basis. But if a relationship is causing permanent damage beyond repair, help me know when to cut that relationship out. I pray this in Jesus' name, amen.

Questions

- What minor injury have you received lately?
- Are you able to forgive easily and give mercy quickly?
- Have you ever unknowingly injured someone you love?

*** Give mercy to receive mercy!***

DAY 8: BROKEN MUSCLE

I deadlifted my max weight. I was supposed to do four reps of this heavy weight, but I wound up only able to do two reps. The third time I tried to lift the barbell stacked with weight on each side, I pushed up with my legs hard against the floor and tightened my core, trying desperately to lift the weight. But the barbell didn't budge. I let go and walked around the gym for a moment to catch my breath and returned to try the deadlift one more time. Again, I pushed, grunted, and activated every muscle in my body (including my neck muscles, which were sore the next day), but nothing happened. My body was done, and every muscle was exhausted. I couldn't lift the weight anymore, but the sheer effort of trying caused my entire backside to be sore.

Most of the time when my muscles are sore, I love a good massage. The massage can be painful, but it does wonders at loosening tight muscles and flushing out the waste material collected from the muscle tearing and healing, which is necessary for muscle growth. Although my entire back was sore, it was my trapezius (traps) and upper rhomboids that hurt the most. I asked my son to gently rub the top part of my back, but the muscles hurt so much that I couldn't stand even the lightest touch. I knew, though, that I had to keep the muscles moving or else the pain would get worse. I kept up my cardio, took hot baths and waited. Only time would take the pain away.

Many times we get hurt in life, and the massage of someone's encouraging words can help abate the soreness. However, sometimes we get hurt so badly that words simply aggravate the pain. In this case, we simply need to keep living day-to-day, soak in God's Word and let time decrease the aching. We want the pain to leave automatically, but that is usually not possible. The pain must work itself out. The stronger the pain, the longer the wait. But we can be encouraged. Our pain will not be wasted. God will use our brokenness to make us stronger if we let Him. We just have to trust Him.

"He heals the brokenhearted and binds up their wounds" (Psalm 147.3 NIV).

Father, I know that you can use the words of others to help heal minor injuries that I experience in this life, but I also know that there are hurts too deep for words. Help me to rest in You when I feel broken beyond repair. Surround me with Your soothing Words from the Bible and other Christian resources. I want the pain to leave now, but I know that I can at least handle the pain if I can rest in You. Hold me in the palm of Your hand. I don't want to give up on life. Help me to stay the course even though everything aches. I trust that the pain won't last long and that joy will soon come (Psalm 30.5). I pray this in Jesus' name, amen.

Questions

- Have you experienced brokenness that words couldn't mend?
- Why is important to keep living life even after a major injury?
- How has God soothed you in your time of need?

Joy will come in the morning!

DAY 9: CARING FOR MUSCLE

I've work out my entire adult life. I love it. If a few days go by and I haven't exercised, I begin to feel frustrated and a little blue. I'm so used to the endorphins and the energy I get when I exercise that it's become a necessary part of my life. Even though I've always exercised, I've only recently (in the last three years) aggressively begun to lift weights. Since I used to only do cardio, my muscles weren't very developed. I didn't have to eat a lot of protein because muscle growth wasn't a big part of my exercise routine. I endeavored to eat healthy, but I didn't need to watch my macronutrients (protein, fats and carbohydrates) as strictly as I do now.

I remember when I wanted to lose a few pounds; I would simply decrease my calories for a while. After a few weeks of strict dieting, two or three pounds would be gone. But now if I want to lose a few pounds, I just can't stop eating. I have much more muscle mass that needs constant calories in order to be maintained. I need to be more creative when I want to lose some extra fat. I have to restrict only a few hundred calories over several weeks and/or add a few extra High Intensity Interval Training sessions during my week. I can't just do whatever I used to do in order to get my desired weight outcome. Having muscle takes attention and care, and I have to account for it when I want to lose weight.

Having muscle resembles someone who has some form of leadership. Whether we are a parent, boss, church leader, etc., we can't just do whatever we want without considering the people whom God has entrusted to us. As a mom, I can't set out to accomplish my goals without considering my family first. I know that there are three precious souls relying on me, and I need to figure my ministry of motherhood into all I do. I can still accomplish my goals—they just may take longer to achieve and I may have to be a little more creative to reach them. God has placed us all in some form of leadership position, and we have to take into account everyone and everything depending on us. Otherwise, we may lose more than we will actually gain.

"Do nothing out of selfish ambition or vain conceit. Rather, in humility value others above yourselves, not looking to your own interests but each of you to the interests of the others" (Philippians 2.3-4 NIV).

Father, help me to count the cost before chasing my destiny. I know that You have great plans for me, but I also know that You have Your perfect will and way. Help me to rest in Your timing and not rush out, trying to achieve my dreams in my own strength. I have people who depend on me, and You care about them just as much as you care about me. I know that I can be creative and patient while I work towards Your promise for my life. I trust that the Holy Spirit will guide me in all truth and righteousness, so I can accomplish ALL the great things You have planned for me. I pray this in Jesus' name, amen.

Questions

- Have you ever chased God's promises in the wrong way?
- How can you creatively work towards your destiny?
- What is God telling you to be patient in today?

Be patient and creative!

DAY 10: BACKSTAGE

Being backstage with so many amazing bodybuilders can be intimidating. I remember looking at everyone thinking that they all looked like first place winners to me. I even found myself comparing myself to a few of the competitors in my division. One woman had bigger biceps and another woman had a leaner overall shape. Comparing myself to others almost killed the joy I had in my own accomplishment to even be able to compete! No matter how hard and how long I worked, there will always be someone that I think is bigger and better than I am. We are all designed with a different shape and physique, and we each have our strengths and weaknesses.

I could spend my time backstage being consumed with comparisons or I could appreciate my strengths and enjoy the process of competing. No matter who won the competition, we all worked hard to get there. Winning a trophy is nice, but it should never be the overall goal for bodybuilding. Our goal is to grow, learn and appreciate the sport. As I looked around at all the competitors, I saw people who had struggled to achieve their goals, and I was honored to be in their company. We each had our reasons for competing, and we all overcame different obstacles to get there. The trophy would go to someone, but win or lose; we each worked hard and performed our best.

Although the trophies of this life are fleeting, there is a heavenly trophy that is everlasting. Jesus will reward each of us according to the work we accomplished for Him on earth. We don't have to compare our work to anyone else because we were each created and called to do something specific and unique. We are each on our own path of victory. God has a reward with our name on it, and He has given us the ability and strength to achieve our goals as we learn to rely on Him. And one day when we meet Jesus face to face, He will see our hard work manifested in us as we step onto center stage in heaven. We will each receive a victor's crown from our Heavenly Father for our work done in obedience to His will on earth.

"For the Son of Man is going to come in his Father's glory with his angels, and then he will reward each person according to what they have done" (Matthew 16.27 NIV).

God, help me to not compare my life and my design to anyone else. I realize that You have created me for a purpose, and I want to serve the need for which I was created. We all have our own reward waiting for us in heaven. Help me not getting discouraged by watching others succeed; rather, let their hard work motivate me to stretch further, learn more and accomplish greater things for Your glory. I know that one day I will appear before You in heaven, and I want to show You the victory I had in Your name on earth. Thank You for giving me the chance to do something great in Your Kingdom. I pray this in Jesus' name, amen.

Questions

- What purpose do you think God is giving you?
- Has God designed you specifically to achieve a purpose?
- Have you ever been discouraged because of comparisons?

Don't compare and keep your joy!

DAY 11: SELF-MASSAGE

Sometimes my muscles become so tight and sore from a particularly difficult workout that I can barely move them. One morning, my shoulder muscles were extremely sore from my workout the previous day that I could barely lift my arms. The tightness made it difficult to write at the computer. I realized that I needed to massage the tender muscles or else I would not be able to fulfill my calling as a writer that day. Finally, I grabbed some massage lotion and sat down on the floor. I knew what I needed to do. I proceeded to gently rub one of my shoulders, loosening the muscle fibers. After the muscle became warm, I then began to really manipulate the muscle, stretching and prodding the sinews of the entire shoulder. Needless to say, the process really hurt, and I wanted to stop several times. But I knew that if I didn't work the tension out of my shoulders, I would not be able to write.

When I was done with one shoulder, I went to the next shoulder. I manipulated the muscle, rubbing my thumbs and finger through the width of my shoulder to the pectoral muscle. When I finally finished both shoulders, I laid back on the ground. I was glad it was over, and I felt so much better. I gained a better range of motion of both arms and the tension had loosened a bit. I went back to my computer and began to write again, relieved that I had done what was good for me even though it hurt.

Many times God calls us to obediently do what hurts. We have tension in our life that will only be resolved if we obediently go through a painful process of restoration and healing. The longer we resist doing what God has called us to do, the longer we must wait before we can do the greater things He has planned for us. Sometimes this means we need to cut stuff out of our schedule. Other times we may need to apologize for previous actions. And maybe God has even called us to go to seek help from others with counseling or coaching. But whatever it is, we must stay committed even when it hurts so bad that we want to give up. The process will eventually be over, and we will be able to rest in our newfound peace and relief.

"For His anger is but for a moment, His favor is for a lifetime. Weeping may endure for a night, But a shout of joy comes in the morning" (Psalm 30.5 AMP).

Father, I don't want to keep avoiding a painful process that you are calling me to because I know it is preventing me from accomplishing the greater things that You have planned for me. Help me to finally overcome my fears and just get the pain over with, so I can move on in peace. I know that the tension will be gone, and I'll finally be able to heal. It is difficult to obediently walk through pain, but I trust that You know what You are doing and You have my best interest at heart. Help me today to make the decision to finally obey what I have been evading for some time. I pray this in Jesus' name, amen.

Questions

- Is there a difficult process that you have been delaying?
- Do you have tension in your life?
- Do you need to seek additional resources to help you?

The pain gives way joy!

DAY 12: EASY AT THE TOP

I use a 45-pound plate weight on both sides of my barbell when I warm up for my squats. After my first set, I begin adding additional plate weights to each side, moving from 135 pounds all the way to about 175 for my fourth set of reps. At my heaviest, when I first lift the barbell from the squat rack, the weight feels manageable. My legs are able to carry the weight easily as long as I don't move too much. It is not until I have to make my legs move into a deep squat position that my body feels the full weight of the 175 pounds on my shoulders. Now the weight feels extremely heavy, and I have to use all my might just to stand up again.

After 8 reps, I am more than happy to put the barbell back onto the squat rack. My chest is heaving, trying to suck oxygen into my lungs as fast as possible. It takes me a full three minutes just to bring my heart rate back down. I find it interesting that the weight can feel so different, depending on the movements of my body. When I barely move, the weight feels light. But when I activate my muscles and make sweeping movements with my body, the weight is almost unbearable. This reminds me a lot of the weight of our God-given promises. Why is it that sometimes the weight doesn't feel so heavy, yet other times the weight of it almost seems suffocating?

I realized that when I'm doing nothing with my promises, distracted by everyday life and responsibilities, I don't notice the weight of God's promises for my life as much. I can almost come to the point where I don't feel the burden of my dreams. However, when I activate my belief and move my faith muscles with God's promises resting on my shoulders, I now suddenly feel the burden God has placed on me. It almost feels too heavy to carry, and I wonder how many reps I'm going to have to do until God finally comes through for me. But I must trust the process of waiting and pushing because I know that God is making me stronger to handle the burden and blessings that come with my promises. I won't give up on my dreams, and I will use every ounce of energy in me to stay committed to what God has claimed over my life.

"Let us not become weary in doing good, for at the proper time we will reap a harvest if we do not give up" (Galatians 6.9 NIV).

Father, I know that You have given me promises for my life, and I will activate my faith and believe in those promises. I know the weight of my destiny may sometimes feel suffocating, but I trust that I'm becoming stronger during my wait. You are making me into the likeness of Your Son, and I won't give into pressure or give up. I will move according to Your will even when the path seems difficult and tedious. Help me not to become weary. I know that when the time is right, You will fulfill Your promises for my life, and I will walk in the fullness of my destiny. I pray this in Jesus' name, amen.

Questions

- Do you feel the weight of God's promises on your life?
- Have you ever been tempted to be impatient?
- What can you do today to activate your faith?

Don't give up on your promises!

DAY 13: AT YOUR WORST

Every sport, talent, ability, gifting, etc. has its shining moments, but they each have their ugly moments too. It feels awesome to be presented on stage in a bodybuilding competition with spray tan, makeup and hair done and all the water weight gone from the body. However, that moment on stage is only as good as all the ugly, grueling, sweat-filled moments that make the great moment possible. I had many ugly moments while I trained for my bodybuilding competition. I cried, complained, panicked and even felt tempted to give up. Training for anything is hard, especially when all energy is consumed with making sacrifices and staying diligent. But I would have never achieved my best on stage if I hadn't gone through my worst at home and in the gym.

When we find ourselves at our worst, we must remember that it will not last long. Every worst has its complimentary best, and God knows that we will get there eventually. We want to be perfect and presentable all the time, but that just isn't possible. There will always be a struggle that is propelling us forward. People who never flounder are people who are good at covering up the ugliness. However, to admit a struggle is to admit that we are learning, stretching and growing.

God is huge on giving mercy. He knows that the human condition is flawed, and we will all struggle to achieve our best in Him. Becoming like Christ is no easy feat, and we will have many ugly moments along the way. There will be times of weakness that will embarrass us later down the road, but we must not be ashamed of our struggle. Instead of carrying guilt, we can extend mercy to ourselves. Same goes with other people. The closer we are to others, the more ugly moments we will see. But instead of judging and criticizing, we can offer mercy and encouragement. Usually, the person will get back up and continue running the course, knowing that there is a shining victory just ahead. Instead of getting stuck in the bad moments, we can relish the great ones at the end of every struggle.

"God blesses those who are merciful, for they will be shown mercy" (Matthew 5.7 NLT).

God, I want to be merciful on myself. I don't want to get caught up in my weakness and mistakes that I miss out on the amazing moments of triumph along the way. I know that I will never be perfect, and I will struggle with the great things You have prepared for me. I will not back down from the fight just because some of the moments are ugly. I won't be embarrassed or ashamed; instead, I will gracefully give and receive mercy. Also, teach me to not judge or criticize people who are going through difficulty. I know that they are achieving great things even if it looks like they're failing at the moment. Help me to encourage those around me and to be a voice of motivation when they are down. I pray this in Jesus' name amen.

Questions

- What is an ugly moment that you've experience in your life?
- How have you struggled to achieve something great?
- Do people see you at your worst or only at your best?

Give mercy and receive mercy!

DAY 14: SODA AND WATER

I had to drink close to 2 gallons of water a day for the 9 months that I trained for my bodybuilding competition. To bring this in perspective, an average bottle of water has 16.9 ounces. One gallon of water has 128 ounces, so two gallons has 256 ounces. So that means I drank around 15 bottles of water a day! That's a lot. That means I had to drink 5 bottles of water every morning, 5 in the afternoon and 5 in the evening. I felt like I was drinking water all of the time. Because of all the water I had to drink, I stopped drinking soda. There was no way I could fit soda in with all the water I was drinking. I chose water when out to eat, during a movie, at the vending machine, while at home, etc. I completely stopped drinking soda, and even now I don't have much taste for it.

So many times, we struggle with the bad habits in our lives. Maybe we watch too much television, or we eat or drink too much at night, or we struggle with a bad relationship or we battle with negative thoughts. Whatever the bad habit is, focusing on it will only make it worse. It is better to fill up with something positive that will disperse the negative. We can start a new hobby, find new friends, listen to interesting podcasts or even start journaling. It's not about ripping out the negative; rather, it's about stuffing ourselves with so much positive that the negative can no longer stay.

Although there are many good activities in the world, the number one way to disperse the bad is to fill up with Jesus. Jesus is the Living Water, and He can disperse all the "empty" calories in our lives. When we consume a lot of Christian media (including podcasts, sermons, books, TV, movies, etc.) and devour the Bible, the ugly thoughts, emotions, behaviors, etc. in our lives will have no choice but to move out. We are called "jars of clay" in the Bible, and just like any container, we can only hold so much. Instead of embracing things that harm us, we can embrace God's Word, which will transform us.

"But we have this treasure in jars of clay to show that this all-surpassing power is from God and not from us" (2 Corinthians 4.7 NIV).

God, I no longer want to focus on the negative things in my life. I trust that You are strong enough to change me little by little as I center my attention on You. I want to consume more of Jesus every day, so the darkness in my life will be dispersed by Your light. I know that if I read more of Your Truth, watch more of Your Truth, listen to more of Your Truth and think on more of Your Truth that I don't have to worry about fighting my battles alone. When I put You as the center of my life, You will fight my battles for me, and I can rest in Your goodness and strength. Help me to realign my world, so that You become the most important thing in it. Only then will the struggles that plague me truly fall away and die. I pray this in Jesus' name, amen.

Questions

- What are you struggling with today?
- Have you exhausted time trying to fight this battle alone?
- How can you consume more of God's Word?

Consume more of God!

DAY 15: FASTING FOOD

Food is one of those things that many Westerners take for granted. Not only do we think we should have food whenever we want it, we think we should be able to have whatever kind of food that we have a craving for. On any given day, we can have Chinese, Italian, Mexican, Middle Eastern or American food, depending on our mood. When much of the world is starving, we are overeating on so much food that it's actually killing us. The largest percentage of deaths in America is due to overeating and obesity. We have the appetites of kings, but the self-control of toddlers. And when we try to diet and control our food intake, we think our world is falling apart. But the truth is that we probably eat more while we are dieting than the people in 3rd world countries eat when they think they're feasting.

One aspect of bodybuilding that I both enjoyed and hated was the fasting. Fasting doesn't necessarily mean saying no to all foods; it can simply mean saying no to certain foods and the amount of food for a specific amount of time. What I found was that I don't have to completely turn my life upside down when I'm fasting certain foods. I simply tweak my food choice a bit. When I cook at home, I make foods for the family that are healthy and we can all enjoy. When I go out to eat, I pick foods that are a part of my diet. When I go to a movie, I'll throw a healthy snack in my purse. I simply wield a little self-control, reminding myself that although I may feel a little deprived, I am still eating better than much of the world.

We all should do a little fasting now and then. It doesn't have to be simply about losing weight or getting healthy. It can be about leaning into the Lord and relying on Him to sustain us. If we don't struggle with food, we can fast other things: alcohol, TV, social media, worry, idleness, etc. We can pray and ask the Holy Spirit to show us where we are being gluttonous and ask for the self-control to fast. Life is too short to allow things and circumstances to control us. We have the mind of Christ and the power of the Most High dwelling in us. There is no reason to let food and other worldly things bully us. We are strong in Christ. We are anointed for great things. We must overcome any areas of gluttony, so God can unleash us to achieve our fullest destiny in His Kingdom.

"For, 'Who can know the LORD's thoughts? Who knows enough to teach him?' But we understand these things, for we have the mind of Christ" (1 Corinthians 2.16 NLT).

God, I don't want to be pushed around by gluttonous actions and attitudes any longer. I know by faith that I have prevailing self-control because You have given me Your power and strength. I want to tap into that self-control, so I can gain some balance in my life. There is nothing wrong with food and things of this world, as long as I control them and they don't control me. Teach me to listen to the Holy Spirit before I let my appetites consume me. I know that You will guide me on paths of righteousness, and I look forward to getting to know and trust You more during my time of fasting. I pray this in Jesus' name, amen.

Questions

- What appetites tend to have control over you?
- How can you start a fasting routine today?
- What reward does God have on the other side of this struggle?

Let God take control!

DAY 16: THIRD PLACE FIGURE

There are four main divisions in women's bodybuilding: Bikini, Figure, Physique and Bodybuilding. Bikini is the leanest of the four divisions with bodybuilding being the most muscular. For my second bodybuilding competition, I competed in four competitions. Three of my competitions were in women's physique. This level is just under bodybuilding and requires larger muscles, using the typical bodybuilding poses, like the double bicep and side triceps poses, to demonstrate strength. I had never competed in physique and it was my main focus for this competition. However, I also decided to compete in one figure competition. I had gotten fifth place in figure the previous year, so I thought it would be fun to try again. Figure is just under physique in muscularity and consists of quarter turn poses on stage.

I have tight shoulders and pectoral muscles, so the "X" form the body is supposed to take in figure has always been difficult for me. My shoulders won't go wide enough, and I can't get my latissimus dorsi muscles (lats) to flare out well. During the award ceremony, I received a 1st place and two 2nd places in the physique divisions. I remember being tired after two long days of the competition process, and I wanted to skip the award ceremony for figure. I doubted I would place, so I thought I should leave to eat and get some rest. Although I was tempted to skip the rest of the event, I forced myself to stay in line and get back on the stage. I knew I needed to finish everything I had committed to. To my surprise, I won 3rd place. I would have completely missed that win if I hadn't stayed to the finish.

Many times our hearts deceive us and try to get us to give up early, but we don't realize that our victory is right around the corner. Just when we feel like giving up is when we need to dig in our heels and hold tight to our commitments. God knows how much we have worked, and He sees how tired we are. Our efforts do not go unseen, and He will bless us for staying the course and not giving up. We just need trust that rest will come soon enough. When we feel emotionally and physically compromised, we must cling onto what we know is right. We must make the decision beforehand that we will follow through everything we committed to no matter how we feel. A trophy with our name on it may be waiting for us if we finish to the end.

"But as for you, be strong and do not give up, for your work will be rewarded" (2 Chronicles 15.7 NIV).

Lord, help me not to give up. I know there are unique situations when You want us to walk away, but for the most part, You tell us to stay strong and to never give up. I pray that I don't let negative feelings and thoughts to cause me to quit. I know that I will struggle in this life to accomplish Your will, but You promise that there will be victory on the other side of my fight. It may not be a trophy made by people, but I trust that Your rewards are far superior to any that the world can give me. I pray this in Jesus' name, amen.

Questions

- Are you in a difficult situation in which you want to give up?
- Is God telling you to let go or lean in and continue the course?
- How can you encourage yourself to stick to God's plan?

Stay the course and win!

DAY 17: THE BODYBUILDER

As I warmed up backstage for my bodybuilding competition, there were whispers about a man close to his 80s who was competing with us. I looked around and instantly saw him. He had grey hair, worn skin and a smile on his face. He was warming up with a couple of dumbbells unaware of all the people staring at him. I would have guessed this man to be in his late 50s to early 60s. The fact that he was almost 80 was awe-inspiring. I had to meet him. I walked straight up to him and introduced myself. He was gracious and listened while I congratulated him on his victory. The victory wasn't a trophy; it was his desire to defy the limitations of age. He set his mind to bodybuilding and didn't let anything stop him.

Later that evening when the man went on stage, everyone rushed out into the audience to watch him compete. He was in the masters' division with only one other competitor. There was about a twenty-year age difference between them, but we couldn't tell. They both looked healthy, vibrant and in shape. Each man posed well, but the older man was enthralling. It was obvious to the audience just how much he enjoyed posing on stage. His grin stretched across his face, and he loved to hear the applause from the crowd. He relished every single moment of the spotlight. It wasn't about winning for him. It was about enjoying the process. I don't know if it was his age or his personality, but he did not take one moment on stage for granted. Every second was special.

Life is short, and God has gifted us with an existence that allows us a certain amount of days on earth. Every single second is special and valuable. We are alive in God's creation, and we will be with Him for eternity. But now He has given us the life on earth to grow and learn. God is so wise and imaginative that He can even use our mistakes to mold us into the image of Jesus. Not a single moment is wasted; and good or bad, we can appreciate each day on earth. And when it's time for us to shine on stage, instead of entertaining an attitude of cowardice or shame, we can soak all of it in—the work, the applause, the satisfaction and the victory. Because we know that the ultimate victory is the Lord's, and we can be found in Him, living out that victory on earth.

"I have told you these things, so that in Me you may have [perfect] peace. In the world you have tribulation and distress and suffering, but be courageous [be confident, be undaunted, be filled with joy]; I have overcome the world." [My conquest is accomplished, My victory abiding]" (John 16.33 AMP).

I want to relish every moment You have given me on earth, God. I realize that You have blessed me in so many ways that I take for granted. Teach me to number my days. Show me the preciousness of each new morning. I want to make a big deal of each day because they are all gifts. Help me to embrace the beauty of Your creation and the wonderment of how You are moving in my life. You want us to enjoy our lives because You love when we are filled with joy and thanksgiving. Today, I thank You for all your many blessings. I pray this in Jesus' name, amen.

Questions

- Do you enjoy your life?
- Do you have blessings that you have taken for granted?
- How can you show God gratitude today?

Treat each day as a gift!

DAY 18: HAIR REDO

I hired someone to do my hair and makeup for my bodybuilding competition. I figured if I was going to work hard for nine months of training, the least I could do was get my hair professionally made up. Since I competed in the physique division, I wanted to have my long hair off my shoulders. I didn't want to have to continually bring my hair to the side when doing back poses. I chose a very pretty French braid across the crown of my head that wrapped into a loose bun at the nape of my neck. I sat in the salon chair and let the stylist perform her hair magic on me. The braid took a while to prepare, but I loved it.

Little did I know that the braid would start unraveling during the first part of my competition. The loose braid was great in theory, but performing all of my poses created too much movement. After the morning competition, I showed up early before the second half and asked the hair stylist to tighten the braid and bun. She added lots more bobby pins and covered my hair with hairspray. I sat in the salon chair one more time and watched in the mirror as the stylist secured my hair to my head. There was no way my hair would fall out this time.

God likes when we have creative ideas, especially when we are undertaking new ventures. The only problem is that when we are doing something new, our great plans may not be practically sound. We may soon experience our precious ideas unraveling. This doesn't necessarily mean that we have to chuck the whole undertaking. Maybe we just need to sit down and "tighten" and "secure" our strategy. God will give us a redo when the course is right but the direction needs to be tweaked a bit. It may take a little time, but making minor adjustments to secure the plan is better than allowing it all to slowly collapse.

"In their hearts humans plan their course, but the Lord establishes their steps" (Proverbs 16.9 NIV).

God, I want to do new things for Your glory. I'm going to do the best I can to stay prepared, but I realize that I will have to make adjustments along the way. I know that just because one of my ideas may unravel, it doesn't mean my course is wrong. When I fall, I simply need to get back up and continue in the right direction. Mistakes are just part of doing something new, and they don't mean that I need to give up on the desires You have placed in my heart. Thank You for making me a creative, innovative person. I dedicate all of my plans to You. Guide me through the process and help me to grow into the person You have created me to be. I pray this in Jesus' name, amen.

Questions

- Are you committing to something new today?
- Have you made mistakes that taught you something?
- What adjustments to the course does God have for you?

Make adjustments on the way!

DAY 19: STUCK ELEVATOR

The morning of my competition started early. I had to meet in another hotel room at 5am to start my hair and makeup. There were many athletes packed in the room, and it took me over an hour to finally sit down in the salon chair. By the time my hair and makeup were complete, I had only 30 minutes to get to the competition venue. I raced to my room to grab my workout bag that held my suit, shoes, snacks and other necessary items. Finally, I got to the elevator and along with five other competitors, waited for it to steadily go down to the first floor. When the elevator arrived at the first floor, the door would not open. We were all stuck.

I was already feeling rushed. The morning started out with plenty of time until the competition, but my makeup and hair delay created a time crunch. Now I was stuck with five other people who were already anxious to get to the competition. I felt my heart begin to pound, and I almost wanted to vent my frustration. But I felt the Holy Spirit quietly tell me that nothing was a surprise to Him. I needed to rest in the confidence that God knew what was going on, and He always has the best plans for me. It only took a short minute for some of the other competitors to start yelling and venting their frustrations with heated language. The small elevator was brimming with negative energy.

I realized quickly that there should be a difference between people who have Jesus in their hearts and people who don't. Jesus is more than willing to take our frustrations, anxiety and worry. In fact, He died to take every little negative thing in our lives. I didn't have to vent my frustration; I only needed to trust God's plan. For some reason, He wanted that elevator to get stuck. Whether I was late or on time didn't matter because God knew what He was doing. Instead of worrying, I simply smiled and waited with a supernatural calm that can only come from knowing Jesus. I wasn't alone. I had the God of the Universe on my side, waiting in that elevator with me. Fifteen minutes later, I watched as crowbar forced the elevator door opened. Never did I lose my cool, and I made it to the competition right on time.

"So do not fear, for I am with you; do not be dismayed, for I am your God. I will strengthen you and help you; I will uphold you with my righteous right hand" (Isaiah 41.10 NIV).

God, I know that I will be in situations that are tense and frustrating, and I want there to be a marked difference in my reaction. I want to have a peace that is supernaturally imparted to me by You. Help me to be a light in the darkness. Teach me how to react to difficult circumstances with love and not fear. I trust that You are always with me everywhere that I go. I don't have to be afraid because nothing surprises You. I hope that the next time I'm in a tense situation that I react according to Your will and not the way of the world. I pray this in Jesus' name, amen.

Questions

- How did you react in a current stressful situation?
- Can you remind yourself that God is always with you?
- Was there a tense time you reacted in fear instead of faith?

Do not fear for God is with you!

DAY 20: POSE PRACTICE

Lifting weights is only one of the many elements of competing in a bodybuilding competition. It would be of no use for me to build muscles if I didn't know how to present them on stage. Since I had never competed in the physique division before, I hired a trainer to help me workout and to learn my poses. For me, the physique poses were fun to learn. They are the movements synonymous with bodybuilding, including the Front Double Bicep Pose, Side Chest Pose, Side Triceps Pose and the Abdominal Pose. These poses do the best job possible to present the development of each muscle group. Otherwise, my hard work would not show. I must not only build strength but also learn how to demonstrate that strength in the correct way.

During my workouts, my trainer would randomly yell out one of my many poses. I would have to drop everything that I was doing and go straight into that pose, holding it while she inspected. I practiced each pose over and over again in front of the mirror until they became like second nature to me. If I did not learn them instinctively, I would have fumbled on stage. The stage does a good job at making one's mind go blank. If the poses are not already there in the competitor's body-memory, she or he will forget how to do them on stage.

There are a lot of Christians who are strong in their faith. They diligently work each day at studying God's Word and listening to the Holy Spirit. However, when asked to display what they have learned, they may become awkward and uncomfortable. They are not relaxed while sharing their faith-knowledge to others because they do not practice sharing it privately. It may sound weird, but we can practice explaining our faith to our families, friends and even to the mirror. The more we become comfortable talking about Jesus and what He did on the Cross for us, the better we will become at explaining our faith in public. We can't just have strong faith that no one can see. We must explain the Gospel over and over again in our hearts until expressing it becomes second nature. When we are called out in public to explain why we believe in Jesus, we can trust that the Holy Spirit will pull just the right words out at the right time, and we will be comfortable explaining what we know is true.

"Instead, you must worship Christ as Lord of your life. And if someone asks about your hope as a believer, always be ready to explain it" (1 Peter 3.15 NLT).

God, I want to be comfortable sharing my faith with others, especially in public places. I desire to be able to drop everything that I'm doing and present the Gospel to whomever is seeking Truth. Help me to not only understand faith for myself, but teach me how to clearly present the Gospel to people who are watching my life of faith. I want talking about my faith to become second-nature to me. I know that You will daily guide me in all Truth and give me everything that I need for each day. Help me to stay diligent in the Word and in communication with You, so I can be ready to explain my life of faith to others. I pray this in Jesus' name, amen.

Questions

- Have you explained your faith to another person?
- Are you comfortable with discussing Jesus with others?
- How can you practice sharing your faith today?

Practice makes perfect!

DAY 21: PROTEIN

Bodybuilding is definitely an art. Although lifting weights is a major player in this sport, food intake is just as important. I remember when I first started lifting, I had no idea what a macronutrient was. Other weightlifters would discuss their "macros," and I knew there was a major element of bodybuilding that I was missing. There are three main macronutrients (macros): proteins, carbohydrates and fats. We must feed our bodies all three macros in specific portions in order to gain mass. Then the macro portions must be adjusted several weeks before competition in order to maintain muscle while also shedding fat. It's a precise science that every bodybuilder will want to learn.

I like to compare each macronutrient for the body to a macronutrient for the spirit. We all want to grow spiritually, but many times we are not feeding our souls the right macronutrients in order to mature and grow. The first macronutrient that is required in bodybuilding is protein. Protein has amino acids, which are the building blocks of the body. Without protein, a bodybuilder cannot grow. I like to compare protein to the Bible and other biblical resources, like devotionals, sermons, Christian books and music, etc. Many Christians want to grow spiritually, but they are not consuming Scripture. God allows each of us to be broken in this life, so we can grow in our faith. But if we are not reading His Word and resources inspired with His Word every day; instead of becoming better, we will become bitter. We must feed our souls portions of God's protein constantly, especially when we are going through a particularly difficult season.

The Bible is not just a chronicle of historical events. The Bible is "alive and powerful," and the Holy Spirit will use God's Word to speak to us personally. God can take spiritual truths from the Bible and apply them directly to our needs and situations. God wants to

49

reveal more of Himself to us, and He will unveil mysteries to us that let us know that He is involved in all aspects of our lives. He wants to pour His revelation into our hearts, minds and spirits, so our faith in His promises will stand firm. It may take time to learn, but we can start consistently reading God's Word and begin receiving His revelations today.

"For the word of God is alive and powerful. It is sharper than the sharpest two-edged sword, cutting between soul and spirit, between joint and marrow. It exposes our innermost thoughts and desires" (Hebrews 4.12 NLT).

Father, guide me in exploring and studying Your Word. I want to grow stronger in my faith, not weaker. And I know that I must read the Bible daily, so I can have enough "protein" to mature in Christ. I understand that the Bible can be confusing at times, and it will take discipline to continue reading it faithfully, but I am willing to learn. You will guide me in all truth, and I believe You have mysteries and revelations to show me. There is so much about You, Lord, that I want to know. More specifically, though, I simply want to know You more intimately. Help me to learn. I pray this in Jesus' name, amen.

Questions

- How often do you read the Bible?
- How can you fit reading God's Word into Your schedule?
- What revelation do you feel God wants to reveal to you today?

Consume God's protein!

DAY 22: CARBOHYDRATE

Carbohydrates are also very important to bodybuilding. They give bodybuilders the energy to lift weights and grow muscle. Without carbohydrates, they would not have the energy to recover and repair broken muscle. I like to compare carbohydrates to prayer and worship. When we worship God and talk with Him, we are filled with a supernatural energy that empowers us to fulfill God's amazing plans for our lives. Without satisfying our lives with God's restorative energy, our spiritual walk may become flat and tired.

When we go to church and sing praises to the Lord in true worship, we fill up on feelings of love and power. We can enjoy this experience outside of our church in the everyday moments of our lives at home, work or wherever we are. We can physically and spiritually sense our souls being replenished with joy, strength and courage. And when we pray to our Heavenly Father, we open ourselves up for Him to pour in His power and anointing into our lives. We can surround ourselves with uplifting worship music or podcasts. We can also slip away like Jesus did and pray to God whenever we feel our energy running low or our courage faltering.

But when people overindulge in carbs and do not apply the energy that the carbs give them, they become overweight with stored-up energy. As Christians, we need to apply the energy that God gives us during prayer and worship. We will ultimately deplete our spiritual energy by encouraging, serving and lifting up others; but God will restore our strength. This way we will stay spiritually fit; rather than spiritually fat. People who bounce from one spiritual high to the next without ever operating in the power they gain can become self-serving and useless in the Kingdom of God. We have to pour out what we've been given, trusting that God will continue to fill us back up to overflowing.

"He gives strength to the weary and increases the power of the weak" (Isaiah 40.29 NIV).

God, I want You to fill me with Your supernatural energy today and every day. I need Your strength and power in order to complete the fullness of the plans that You have for me. I want to use up that energy doing Your will and serving others, so I can be filled up again. Show me how to gain energy by worshipping You and communing with You through prayer. Pour Your anointing on me, so I have the power to achieve victory as I walk by faith. I want to be a spiritually vigorous part of Your Kingdom. I pray this in Jesus' name, amen.

Questions

- How can you worship God today?
- Can you break away several times a day to pray with God?
- How is your spiritual fitness?

Stay spiritually fit!

DAY 23: FAT

Fat is a sign of extra. When people have storage of fat on their bodies, they can last days of famine because their bodies will start to break down the fat when food is no longer available. Fat is a necessary part of bodybuilding—both eating healthy fats and storing fat on the body. Eating healthy fats aids the body in absorbing certain nutrients and helps cell growth among other things. Allowing a healthy percentage of fat on the body will permit a bodybuilder to grow muscle. If the body is constantly starving, it will be difficult become stronger because the body is constantly in a calorie deficit.

Although fat needs to be shed several weeks before competition, the time of "bulking" before the time of "cutting" is extremely important. While having too much fat can be damaging, the body does need the right amount of fat in order to safely build muscle mass. The same goes with having "spiritual fat," or what I like to call "spiritual overflow." Christians need this spiritual overflow in order to serve others. The Bible says that Jesus came to give us life in abundance, so we can accomplish all that God has planned for us. Christians who are spiritually starving cannot be used well by God. If they are having trouble feeding themselves, it will be difficult to feed the people around them. Only Christians who have an overflow of God's goodness can go onto share from the wellspring of the Holy Spirit within them.

We must seek to have that overflow, so we can pour out what we are learning onto our families, friends and spheres of influence. We can't only focus on feeding ourselves. We want to be so full of God's Spirit that we must serve others in order to use what we've been given. *Ministry* means to serve. Our ministry is all around us as we serve the people who God has placed in our midst. As we consume God's

53

Word, His Plan and His Spirit, we can share from the abundance within us. However, if our lives are constantly depleted of God, we won't be able to serve the people around us with His goodness and grace. We need that Spiritual fat, so we can "abound in every good work."

"And God is able to bless you abundantly, so that in all things at all times, having all that you need, you will abound in every good work" (2 Corinthians 9.8 NIV).

God, I want You to help me gain some spiritual fat, so I can serve the people around me. I desire to abound in every good work as I fulfill my calling on earth. I need You to bless me abundantly while I faithful seek You and Your Word. I claim the peace of Jesus that is not based on circumstance. I pray that You use me, Lord. I want my actions to have eternal purpose, so my heavenly home will be filled with fruit of my faithfulness to You. I pray this in Jesus' name, amen.

Questions

- Do you have some spiritual fat in your life?
- What are you able to do to serve the people around You?
- What can you do to prevent a spiritual deficit?

It's time to bulk up!

DAY 24: OATMEAL

Towards the end of my competition preparations, my food choices were becoming quite limited. One morning, I made a huge pot of steel cut oats for my family. I was going to put the leftovers in the fridge and eat a small portion from it every morning. I couldn't wait! Just as I was about to pour me a fresh, hot bowl of oatmeal, my trainer texted me. She let me know that oatmeal was no longer on my menu for the last two weeks of competition. I became so upset. I had been looking forward to eating oatmeal since it was one of the only few carbohydrates I had left. But now I had to say goodbye to oatmeal for now. I remember almost wanting to give up. Although oatmeal seems like such a small thing, it felt huge to me since I was already sacrificing so much. Finally, I prayed and the Holy Spirit talked me off the ledge. He reminded me of the bigger plan He was accomplishing in my life.

When God is accomplishing something big in our life, it is easy to get frustrated over little things when we are making great sacrifices. Satan wants us to give up, so he tries to get our attention away from the bigger picture and onto the details. We have to keep our thoughts on the overarching plot that God is moving into place. Giving up on my competition over oatmeal seems funny now, but at that moment I was so emotionally weak from sacrifice. I had to constantly refocus my perspective on why I was competing in the first place: to challenge myself to grow and learn.

When God is doing something big in our lives that takes a lot of sacrifice, we must have a firm understanding of what God is trying to accomplish. If we don't have a greater purpose for our sacrifice, it will be too easy to give up. From the start, we must identify the God's Higher Purpose, so we can remind ourselves over and over again when things get tough. Achieving victory takes hard work and sacrifice, and we can get caught up in the small details if we are not careful. Instead of focusing on what I couldn't have, I needed to remind myself of the gift of health God had given me. Once I surrendered the details (including my oatmeal) to the Holy Spirit, I was able to make the necessary sacrifices, knowing that in just a few short weeks that I would accomplish the victory.

"But you, be strong and do not let your hands be weak, for your work shall be rewarded!" (2 Chronicles 15.7 NKJV).

God, help me not to get lost in the small details of the awesome plan that You are achieving through me. I want to constantly keep my eyes on the bigger picture, so I won't get discouraged by the little sacrifices it takes along the way. I know that great victories take great sacrifices, and I choose not to give-up when I am so close to the finish line. I realize that these sacrifices are not forever, and I can remain strong in the grace that You are pouring out onto me during this difficult time. Remind me of Your overarching purposes today. I trust that You always have eternal rewards for my obedience. I pray this in Jesus' name, amen.

Questions

- Is God trying to accomplish something great in you?
- What sacrifices are beginning to wear you down?
- What is God's purpose in your frustration and pain?

God has an overarching plot!

DAY 25: VACATION

After my bodybuilding competition, my family and I went on vacation. We planned a tropical retreat right after I signed up to be a bodybuilding competitor again. I knew that the competition would be stressful, and I would be worn out from months of training. I wanted a weeklong break from working out, scrutinizing my diet and practicing my routine and poses. Two days after my competition, we were on our way to Hawaii. There is nothing like a long vacation after months of hard work and diligence. I think that the sacrifice and effort leading up to the vacation made the time off even sweeter.

While on vacation, every bite of food I consumed tasted amazing. Being able to lounge at the beach all day without worrying about heading to the gym felt so relaxing. I didn't have to count my macros, worry about sore muscles or practice my poses. Needless to say, this was one of the most memorable vacations that I have ever enjoyed. Every moment was a gift. I simply rested and relished each day. God knows that there will be difficult challenges in our lives, which is why He will allow us times of rest after long stretches of hardships. But shouldn't miss the rest because we feel guilty about slowing down.

The Christian walk of faith can be compared to a journey. Sometimes we will walk through meadows and other times we will walk over mountains. If we don't learn to rest after strenuous uphill climbs, we will eventually tire out and give up. We must take every opportunity that God gives us to rest our bodies, souls and minds. If we are constantly moving, we may actually start to plow in the wrong direction. We must have time to reflect on what really matters and examine our surroundings. All bodybuilders know to allow their hearts and bodies to recuperate after a particularly heavy lift. The heart rate needs to come back down before trying to lift heavy again.

As Christians, we need to let our spirits recuperate after a particularly heavy burden that God has asked us to carry. When we have rested, we will find that we have more energy and strength to continue on the path that God has called us to.

"Come to me, all you who are weary and burdened, and I will give you rest. Take my yoke upon you and learn from me, for I am gentle and humble in heart, and you will find rest for your souls. For my yoke is easy and my burden is light" (Matthew 11.28-30 NIV).

God, help me to learn to rest in You. I know there are moments when You want me to work hard and give all I've got. But there are also other moments when You want me to sit back and rest for a time. Don't let me miss any opportunity that You are giving me to rest. I want the energy and stamina to continue on this faith-journey that You have called me to. I want to embrace the rest You have ordained for me, especially after a very difficult season in my life. Help me to work hard, but also help me to rest and heal. I know that climbing mountains can wear me out and maybe even cause injury, so I want to be completely rested and healed before continuing on my way. I pray this in Jesus' name, amen.

Questions

- Did you ever miss a time of rest that God has given you?
- Do you sometimes confuse resting with laziness?
- After a difficult time, have you enjoyed a moment of peace?

Find rest in God!

DAY 26: LIFT LINGO

I learned quickly that bodybuilding has its own lingo. Words like "swole," "shredded," "cutting," "bulking" and "macros" were all new to me. Also, words that I was familiar with were now being used in different contexts. For example, doing a "negative" meant using the eccentric or muscle lengthening contraction in an exercise move. I remember feeling like I was learning a new English dialect when walking into the gym—almost like I was in another part of the world where English was spoken in a dissimilar way. I gained a lot of new vocabulary during the two years that I competed, including exercise names, muscle vocabulary, health terms and gym slang. And getting certified in Personal Training and Fitness Nutrition opened a whole new world of health science in my life.

Most people at the gym were more than willing to help clarify or explain new terms. They would see the lost look on my face and give me a quick debriefing of what they meant. Some words like "glutes," "pecs," and "hams," were easy to learn and assimilate. However, more complex terms, like "training to failure," "drop setting" and "high intensity internal training," took me longer to understand and apply. I remember how confused I felt during my time of growing as a bodybuilder when I meet new Christians. New Believers who did not grow up in the church and are unfamiliar with church lingo may feel like they too are in another country, listening to English spoken in a very unique way. The life of faith is now opened to them, and they are growing as a young Christian just like we all must do.

Christians who are used to church and church lingo should take care when chatting with new Believers or seekers. This doesn't mean we water down our beliefs, but it does mean we can be aware that others might not understand our lingo. The Holy Spirit does a good job at opening a person's heart to spiritual truths, and all we need to do is express clearly our words without condescension or judgment. It takes us all some time to learn something new, and faith is something that we will be growing throughout our lives on earth. We can show mercy to each other as we make our way down that faith-paths God has us on. Just like the bodybuilders in the gym who took me under their wing, we can encourage and guide those who are new to faith in Jesus Christ.

"Oh, the depth of the riches of the wisdom and knowledge of God! How unsearchable his judgments, and his paths beyond tracing out!" (Romans 11.33 NIV).

God, open my mind to the richness of Your wisdom and knowledge. I want to know You more and seek You more fervently. Also, guide me to be tender and full of grace when speaking with people who are new Believers to faith. I don't want to gloss over spiritual truths; rather, I want to express them in a way that is relevant and tangible to them. I know that we are all a work-in-progress. I pray that I will never be critical of where others are on their walks of faith. Help me to offer mercy and kindness to others and to myself. I pray this in Jesus' name, amen.

Questions

- Do you remember a time when faith was new to you?
- How can you help those around you in their Christian walk?
- Do you have a personal faith story that you can share?

Encourage others in the Lord!

DAY 27: LONG TERM GAINS

When I first started lifting weights, I wanted instant results. I wanted cut biceps, bulging traps, massive quads and a defined six-pack right away. However, just like any sport, no victory comes quickly and easily. First, I had to get rid of my muscle imbalance. My back was weaker than my chest from many years of doing pushups while neglecting my back. And my biceps seemed almost non-existent. Second, I had to build muscle mass. Building muscle mass doesn't happen overnight. It takes months and years of breaking muscle, feeding muscle and repairing muscle to properly grow it. I would get so discouraged when I compared myself to where I wanted to be or to where others were. But I needed to remember that I was just starting out, and I needed to speak positively over the gains I was making.

Fast forward two years later, and I'm still training. Now I can finally see all the improvements that I wanted from the beginning. The only problem is that I can still see areas of improvement. There will always be parts of my body that I want to get leaner or bigger or more cut. The cycle never ends. Improvements can always be made. However, now I don't let myself get discouraged. I know that bodybuilding is a process like anything else. I'm not where I want to be yet, but I'm definitely not where I was. I have improved and that is what counts. My efforts are making a difference. The same is true for our spiritual fitness. Many times Christians want to be spiritual powerhouses right away, but spiritual maturity takes time.

I used to compare myself to other Christians and try to be like them. But I didn't have the spiritual maturity yet to keep up with them. Instead of enjoying where I was on my spiritual journey, I was constantly striving to be more than I was ready for. I wasn't enjoying my life because I was too hard on myself. But just like muscle mass takes time to grow, spiritual mass also takes time. God must break us, feed us His Word, repair us and grow us; and the process of spiritual maturity doesn't happen overnight. There is no rushing it. Instead of being hard on ourselves, we can rejoice in how much we have grown. We may not yet be where we want to be, but we are definitely not where we were.

"Instead, we will speak the truth in love, growing in every way more and more like Christ, who is the head of his body, the church" (Ephesians 4.15 NLT).

God, help me to not be so hard on myself. I want to trust that You are growing me to maturity every day as I seek You, Your will and Your Word. Shape me into the image of Jesus, making slow, solid changes each day. I know that there is much about me that needs improvement, but I also know that I am growing every day. I can see changes in my life from when I began to live for You. Give me Your grace throughout my day, so I can extend that grace to others. I want to enjoy the process of becoming like You, knowing that You will accomplish Your will in my life. I pray this in Jesus' name, amen.

Questions

- Is there an area of your life that needs improvement?
- Do you find yourself comparing yourself to others?
- What areas of your life have you gained strength?

Slow gains are lasting!

DAY 28: THE STAGE MANAGER

One of the workers of the competition was extremely rude to the competitors. He managed the stage, and his every remark reeked with condescension. He had a place of authority in the competition, and instead of using it to impart encouragement to the competitors, he used his platform to wield a boorish control over others. Watching him boss people around in his sharp, sarcastic tone became like darts of negativity that I had to dodge. His remarks were directed at me many times, and I had to ignore his insults and continue smiling. I couldn't let his negative behavior justify me forgetting who I was in Christ. I am a "royal priest" of the Most High God, and I would not behave like someone I was not—even when provoked.

After the first competition and before the second one, I went back to my hotel to eat and take a nap. I happened to see the rude stage manager in the elevator. He was surprised and uncomfortable to see me. He no longer had authority over me outside of the stage, and I could tell he didn't know how to act. He couldn't rudely boss me around in the elevator, so he simply made a snarky joke and tried to avoid eye contact. He seemed like a different person off the stage than he was on the stage. I, on the other hand, behaved exactly the same, and he could tell. My conduct was guided by truth, not an earthly title or positon. I continued to smile and be respectful. I wouldn't respond defensively because I cling tightly to the truth that I am loved by God.

It is easy for Christians to get caught up in human emotions. Yes, we can be treated unfairly, but it is up to us to take offense or not. There are people in the world who are not guided by truth, and they don't have the same moral compass that we have. However, their disrespectful conduct does not justify our own. There is nothing wrong with standing up for ourselves in situations where it is necessary. But as in the instance of the stage manager, he simply wanted to wield the little power he had, and I just needed to get over it. God had bigger plans for me, and I had to keep an eternal perspective. Rather than waste my energy getting upset over something small, I was able to free up my mind to focus on the rest of my competition.

"A person's wisdom yields patience; it is to one's glory to overlook an offense" (Proverbs 19.11 NIV).

God, help me not to take offense to every little rude remark and condensing tone that comes my way. I don't want my mind to be overtaken by the negative actions of others. I want to stay focused on You, God, and the great things You are accomplishing in and through me. I understand that people may behave in ways that I don't like— just like I may have my own bad days. I want to offer grace to others while behaving in a way that honors You at all times. The negative actions of others never justify negative actions being produced in my own life. Guide me in all Truth and let my actions always following the moral standard that You have set. I pray this in Jesus' name, amen.

Questions

- Have you been insulted lately?
- Were you able to continue to behave in an honorable way?
- Have you ever fell victim to the negative emotions of others?

It's for your benefit to overlook offense!

DAY 29: ROLLERS ON A FRIDAY

The evening before my competition, we got to the hotel for the check-in. I got all my forms signed and collected my competition number badge. Next I had to get my first of three spray tans, and then I headed to one of the rooms to get my hair rolled for the next morning. By the time my family and I left for dinner, I had a layer of thick, dark spray tan on me. I was wearing all black to avoid staining my clothes. And I had rollers in my hair. I must have been a sight to behold at the restaurant. I sat down with my family at the table and avoided all the stares. I'm sure the opinions of me varied depending on the onlooker's awareness of bodybuilding competitions. Probably a few people understood my predicament, but everyone else must have thought I was crazy to be looking like I did out in public on a Friday night.

Since there was nothing I could do to explain my situation to strangers, I happily ate my seasoned steak, sweet potato and salad. I knew that the next day would be long and tiring, so I wanted to enjoy the calm before the storm. My family understood the situation, so I enjoyed their company, feeling comfortable in their presence. They were like a protectant shield from all the people around me who couldn't possibly understand what I was doing. Many times as Christians, God puts us into situations that don't make sense to others. He has us take steps of faith that seem odd in the natural. Onlookers may be tempted to judge or criticize us because they don't understand the situation.

Thankfully, during these times of enormous faith, God will usually surround us with a small group of people who understand what we are going through. When Peter asked to walk on water, he was surrounded by the other disciples who saw the entire situation take place. Instead of trying to force Peter to stay in the boat (what makes sense in the natural), they watched him take supernatural steps of the impossible. They may not have walked on water with Peter, but they didn't judge, criticize or discourage his steps of faith (Matthew 14.22-33). God will send us these people when we need them. Though they may not be able to walk out on the stage with us, they will definitely support us with their assuring presence.

"Therefore, since we are surrounded by such a huge crowd of witnesses to the life of faith, let us strip off every weight that slows us down, especially the sin that so easily trips us up. And let us run with endurance the race God has set before us" (Hebrews 12.1 NLT).

God, I realize that not everyone will understand the faith-steps I will take in obedience to Your will. I will not let the uninformed opinions of others to throw me off from the course that You have set before me. I trust that You will surround me with a small group of supporters who will understand what I'm going through. What I am doing may not make sense in the natural, but I trust that You have a supernatural plan that will further Your Kingdom. I'm ready to walk wherever You lead. I pray this in Jesus' name, amen.

Questions

- Has God sent you on an assignment that didn't make sense?
- Did you feel the judgmental stares of others?
- How has your group of supporters help you stay the course?

Surround yourself by witnesses!

DAY 30: PERSONAL TRAINER

Hiring a personal trainer for my bodybuilding competition greatly improved my chances of placing well. Although I am a certified personal trainer myself, I wanted to train with someone who had experience in competing in the physique division. My trainer had competitive information and experience that she gradually imparted to me during our nine months of training. Not only did she teach me, but she helped me lift more in a smaller amount of time. With someone constantly over my shoulder, I find myself lifting heavier, moving faster and working harder than I would alone.

People many times would tell me that they would like to compete, but that they didn't have the time. Or they would look at me and say, "Wow, you must spend five hours in the gym every day." But the truth was that with my trainer, I was only spending an hour a day lifting weights. It wasn't until the last month of my competition that I started throwing in an extra 30-minute cardio routine. But really even an hour and half a day is not much compared to how much time I spend doing other things, like writing, cooking for my family and spending time with my husband. The Holy Spirit is much like a personal trainer. When we give Him a small portion of our day— reading God's Word and spending time with Him—He will ensure that we can do more than we ever thought we could.

Giving God a portion of our day focuses our efforts and keeps us on track with what is truly important. We can get lost in all the pressures and demands that eat away at us each day, but when we learn to rest in God and rely on His timing, we will find that we have all the time we need to finish everything He has called us to achieve that day. People may look at our lives and think we have it easy. They may assume that we simply have more time than they do, but the truth is that everyone has 24 hours every day. When we allow God to be our own Personal Trainer, we will find that we do more than we could have ever thought or imagine when we stay obedient to His plan. God created us and wants us to make the most of this life that He has blessed us with. Only He can guide us on the best and most abundant paths.

"In all your ways acknowledge Him, and He shall direct your paths" (Proverbs 3.6 NKJV).

God, I want you to be the Personal Trainer of my life. Help me to rely on You each day, so I can accomplish more with You than I could alone. I trust that You see what I cannot see and You know what I do not know. I want to lean on Your wisdom and will, so I can achieve many victories for Your glory on this earth. I realize that I have only one life and only 24 hours in each day, so I dedicate a small portion of it each day. I trust that You will guide my every step, making sure that I accomplish everything You have set out for me before time began. I pray this in Jesus' name, amen.

Questions

- Do you take time to spend with God and read the Bible?
- How can you make more time to let God direct your day?
- Have you been able to accomplish more when resting in God?

Let God be your Personal Trainer!

DAY 31: BULKING

One of the most difficult aspects of bodybuilding for me may sound strange to some people. I had trouble eating so much food! Since I was training for the physique division, I had to put on a lot more muscle. This meant that I needed to eat a lot of healthy food, especially protein. Eating over 140 grams of protein a day became burdensome. Also, eating so frequently throughout the day, ensuring that I got the right amount of fats, proteins and carbs, meant that I spent a lot of time preparing food and eating it. Muscle is a liability to the body (it burns energy simply to maintain it), and it will only grow when the body is confident that it is being fed well. If there isn't enough fuel to feed the torn muscle fibers, the body will begin to break down rather than build up.

Although I did use a lot of the energy from the food that I was consuming to build muscle, much of the extra calories were stored as fat. I gained almost ten extra pounds of weight at the height of my bulking period. About half of that weight was muscle and the other half was fat. I couldn't worry about the fat, though. If I were to try to lose the weight too early, I would have never built the muscle I needed for the physique division. I realized that the time for cutting would come soon enough, so I needed just to enjoy the extra calories while they lasted and let my body put on the muscle.

God sometimes will put us through a spiritual bulking period. Maybe He'll have us join a Bible study or give us a steady supply of books to read. Or maybe we'll feel led to consume as many sermons via Podcasts or YouTube as possible. Or we can find ourselves being mentored for a season by someone who imparts great amounts of spiritual guidance to us. Whatever it is, we should take it all in. God sees that a "cutting season" is up ahead—something in our life that

69

will cause us to sacrifice—so He wants to build up as much strength in us as possible. When that bulking season comes upon us, we should listen to God and obey His will. He only wants the best for us, so He is trying to prepare us with all the tools we need to be victorious in the future.

"Now may the God of peace—who brought up from the dead our Lord Jesus, the great Shepherd of the sheep, and ratified an eternal covenant with his blood—may he equip you with all you need for doing his will. May he produce in you, through the power of Jesus Christ, every good thing that is pleasing to him. All glory to him forever and ever! Amen" (Hebrews 13.20-21 NLT).

God, when I sense that You are leading me into a time of spiritual bulking, help me to obey Your direction. I know that You simply want to prepare me for what's to come, so I want to consume as much of Your Word as possible. I don't want to be so busy and exhausted that I don't have the necessary time and energy that is needed to strengthen myself in You. Help me to look at how I'm spending my time, and show me the areas that I need to change in order to consume Your Word and spend time with You in prayer. I pray this in Jesus' name, amen.

Questions

- Describe a season when you consumed a lot of God's Word.
- What did God teach you during your spiritual bulking time?
- Do you find that you are too busy to spend reading the Bible?

Taste and see that the Lord is good!

DAY 32: CUTTING

The cutting period during competition preparation feels like a swift kick. It's a lot of sacrifice squeezed into around six weeks. After I've gained all my muscle, I had to get rid of the extra fat, so the muscle could show. It doesn't matter how much muscle I have gained if the judges can't see it. Over a six-week span, I had to cut many foods out of my diet until the final week when my diet was extremely limited. During the final week, I only ate chicken or salmon with no seasoning, grapefruit, asparagus and a few other green veggies and maybe a little bit of sweet potato. Yes, the cutting period was difficult, but the light at the end of the tunnel was just around the corner, so the sacrifice was bearable.

Once I cut all of my weight, I was so surprised by how well my muscles showed. Every muscle was distinct, and I could see the improvements in each muscle group. Although "show weight" is not maintainable for long, the sacrifices that I was making demonstrated all of my hard work over the past nine months. My determination and efforts were displayed on my physical body. When God allows us to go through a "cutting" or difficult season; instead of focusing on the negatives, we can take this opportunity to show our strength. God does not promise that our lives will be easy, but He does say that He will give us a way to stand strong.

People are watching us, especially when difficult times arise in our lives. It's easy to say God is good when we are enjoying our circumstances, but to say God is good during hard times takes faith. The cutting season in our lives is the time when people can really see our strength. They realize that all the worldly circumstances of happiness have been taken from us for a time, and they want to see if we are strong in the Lord. If our joy comes from the Lord, we can walk in peace no matter the situation. When we are rooted securely in Christ, nothing can knock us out of God's hands. God will not allow the cutting season to last for long, but He will use it to reveal our faith in Him to the world.

"No temptation has overtaken you except what is common to mankind. And God is faithful; he will not let you be tempted beyond what you can bear. But when you are tempted, he will also provide a way out so that you can endure it" (1 Corinthians 10.13 NIV).

God, I know that cutting seasons will occur in my life, and I want my faith to be strong in You. I don't want to feel defeated by my circumstances. Instead, I want all the time I spend in Your Word and with You in prayer to become obvious in my peace and joy that aren't based on circumstances. I hope that when people look at my struggle that they will see someone who is confident in Christ. I want to use my hardships as an opportunity to demonstrate my faith and trust in You and in the Work of Jesus Christ in my life. Although I don't desire hard times or enjoy them when they come, I will stand strong in Your Word because I know I can endure anything for a season with You on my side. I pray this in Jesus' name, amen.

Questions

- Have you been through a difficult season in life?
- Were you able to stand strong or did you fall apart?
- How did God help you through the hard times?

God will provide a way to endure!

DAY 33: MAKEUP

Getting my makeup professionally done was interesting. I was in awe of what an actual artist could do on a clean slate of a face. I have almond shaped eyes, so she made them look even bigger and more slanted. They almost looked otherworldly to me. I enjoyed looking at the final product in the mirror and comparing myself to my usual look throughout my normal day at home. Since I'm a stay-at-home writer, I wear pajamas to my "office" and wear no makeup. I sit at the computer for hours, working my mind and imagination and paying no attention to how I look physically. When I'm done writing, I change into workout clothes (sometimes I'll even workout in my pajamas), and I lift weights and do cardio. When I'm done working out, I'll shower and put pajamas back on if I know that I'm not going anywhere.

The only time I dress in normal clothes and wear makeup is when I run errands. My husband and I have a date night once a week, so I make sure to dress up and look nice for him. My husband has seen me in my most basic environment at home and he has seen me in full makeup and with my hair done on stage. He loves me when I'm plain and when I'm glamorous. Although I enjoy dressing up for him and looking great, he doesn't mind when I wear pajamas and type at my computer. Because in all honestly, I don't want the pressure of always having to look perfect. So often, we as Christians feel this need to be perfect all the time. There is this pressure that since we are Christ-followers that we can't have any flaws. So instead of just being ourselves, we begin to put on a façade of perfection.

But we aren't perfect which is why we reached out for Jesus in the first place. Jesus is our Perfect Substitute. Jesus gives us His perfection and takes our sin, so we can have a relationship with a

Holy God. If we were always perfect, we wouldn't need a Mediator and a Savior. We don't have to hide our flaws and imperfections. We don't have to pretend that we never mess up. We simply need to be who God created us to be: a person with strengths and weaknesses, a person who is not perfect but who is being perfected. I want to be comfortable with myself when I'm glamorous on stage and when I'm plain at the computer. I know that I am loved—mind, soul, body and spirit—and I don't have to prove my worth to anyone.

"But God demonstrates his own love for us in this: While we were still sinners, Christ died for us" (Romans 5.8 NIV).

God, I know that I can be comfortable in who I am and where I am on my faith-journey. You have plans for me that are filled with meaning and purpose, so I will walk in obedience to Your plan. I let go of trying to be perfect, and I cling on to Jesus' Finished Work on the Cross. Thank You for loving me so much that You would die to save me. I want my life to be pleasing to You, so help me follow Your commands and Your will. I offer the plain and glamorous parts of my life to You. I trust that You will always love me no matter what. I pray this in Jesus' name, amen.

Questions

- When do you feel plain and when do you feel glamorous?
- Do you feel like God loves you more when you are good?
- Do you try to earn God's love and favor?

Jesus is your Perfect Substitute!

DAY 34: SUIT CHOICE

One of the fun aspects of a bodybuilding competition is picking out the suit. There are so many colors and fabrics to choose from. Although there are standards in the suit design that every competition requires, the competitors have a great amount of creative license to envision and create a suit that is unique to their individual taste and personality. Many people will try to add limits to suit creativity. They'll say that certain colors and patterns work better for judging, but really that aspect of judging is subjective and cannot be predicted. If competitors are going to spend the money to have a suit made, they should get something that they like and feel comfortable in and not worry about what they think the judges may like or dislike.

My suit choice was simple, and although I think it matched my personality, I do not believe it changed my position on stage. I achieved a first-place, two second-places and a third-place trophy in the four divisions that I competed in, and my suit color and design would not have changed those victories. I was comfortable and felt good in what I wore. The color and design were simply a matter of opinion. God has a specific plan for our lives, but He does give us creative license to fill in the colors and patterns along the way. Yes, there are some things that God specifically requires, but there are other things that are a merely a matter of opinion. These creative details that are part of our purpose won't cause us to lose or achieve the goals that God has place in our hearts—they simply decorate our journey along the way.

As Christians, we can feel like there is a strict design and/or color that our lives must adhere to. But God has designed each of us uniquely, and there is no cookie-cutter pattern to living out the Christian life. We may believe that every little detail has the ability to make or break us. However, I believe that God likes when we are creative, and He does give us creative license within the parameters of His Law and His Divine Plan for our lives. God created us in His image, and He gave us the talents, abilities and imagination to create for His glory. He may have a certain destiny for us, but we can bring the vision to fruition in our own beautiful way.

"So God created human beings in his own image. In the image of God he created them; male and female he created them" (Genesis 1.27 NLT).

God, help me to be more confident and creative in the areas of my destiny that You have given me authority over. I know that You created me with a unique personality and a special design, and I want to demonstrate my imagination in the details of my life and faith. I trust that You have a special purpose just for me, and I look forward to coloring that purpose with my own unique style. Show me the areas in which You have given me creative license, and help me to express myself to the world. I want to be a living piece of art for You, Lord. I pray this in Jesus' name, amen.

Questions

- Are you nervous about being creative within your purpose?
- What is one detail of your life that you can make unique?
- Do you have fear or faith in your God-given imagination?

Use your God-given imagination!

DAY 35: FRIEND PRESSURE

Several of my good friends surprised me by going to my bodybuilding competition. They drove hours to the event, made signs in my honor and brought me yummy after-competition snacks. I was overwhelmed with gratitude that they would spend the money, time and effort to support me. Suddenly, I felt this pressure to do well. I began to think that if my friends made the sacrifice to come watch me compete, I needed to be worthy of their support. I didn't want to let anyone of them down or else their efforts would have been done in vain. I almost regretted them coming because of the pressure I felt to make them proud of me.

I confessed my feelings to one of my friends, and I could tell right away that my thoughts were wrong. I was acting out of insecurity. My friends were supporting me simply because they loved and valued me. They were happy that I placed well, but my placement didn't change their main reason for supporting me. I realized how much I base my self-worth on what I do instead of who I am. I am a wife, mom, sister, daughter and friend, and my existence has value because God created me and placed His seal on me. Although I enjoy achieving victories for His glory, my actions don't change how much God loves me. He loves me simply because He is a God who loves His precious creation.

Culturally, we put so much of our self-worth into our achievements. Although God wants us to excel and do great things, our actions do not place more or less value on us. We have worth because God says we do. God loves and cherishes each of us. He made us in His image and died to redeem us from our sins. He pursues us, and enjoys our company without the awards, acclaim or achievement. Instead of working out of a pressure to earn my worth, I need to work out of the understanding that I have worth already placed inside of me. And whether I win or lose doesn't matter. I am a child of God who is valued, cherished, loved and full of promise and purpose.

"*Now He who establishes us with you in Christ and has anointed us is God, who also has sealed us and given us the Spirit in our hearts as a guarantee*" (2 Corinthians 1.21-22 NKJV).

God, I want to truly know how much I am loved by You. I realize now that Your love for me is not based on my own actions. It is rooted in a supernatural love that cannot be explained or examined in the natural. God, You are Love. You have created me before time began, and You have placed Your seal of approval on me. You love me despite my actions. Help me to fully understand how much I am loved. I want to not only know it in my mind, but I want that realization to sink deep within my heart. I want my eyes to be opened to Your love, and I want my actions to spring from the belief in that love. I pray this in Jesus' name, amen.

Questions

- Do you base your self-worth on your achievements?
- Do you feel uncomfortable receiving God's love?
- Will you accept the truth that you are loved no matter what?

You are loved by God!

DAY 36: WALKING ON STAGE

Going on stage in a suit and spray tan can be intimidating. In fact, it is one of the most vulnerable things that I've ever done. I have to walk out on stage in front of an audience and judges and allow them all to analyze and rate every physical detail of my body. One of the first things I learned when competing was to smile and be confident. If I were to go out on stage, acting like I wasn't good enough and feeling insecure, the judges would most likely agree with me. Somehow, I have to muster the attitude that I own the stage, and I must demonstrate a complete confidence in my bodybuilding efforts.

The only problem is that I'm horrible at faking stuff. I can't act like I own the stage when I feel like I'm equal to all of the other competitors. Instead of trying to act like I'm the best, I simply chose to walk out in grace. Grace is an amazing word that all Christians should understand and embrace. Grace tells us that we don't have to be perfect to be confident. Grace allows us to be aware of both our weaknesses and strengths, yet still feel secure in who we are in Christ. Grace lets me walk out on stage with a smile, knowing that I worked my hardest and I'm valued and loved no matter the outcome. Grace frees me to truly enjoy the stage and offer a smile that is genuine.

We all have metaphorical stages that we must walk onto in life. There will be many occasions when we find ourselves in front of an audience and judges who want to see if we are confident. As Christians, our confidence can be based on an unchangeable and all-powerful God. If we base our confidence on ourselves, we will be a like a ship being tossed about by the waves. However, if we base our confidence on the Finished Work of Jesus, we will be like a firm lighthouse on a hill, spreading light to everyone around us. Because of grace, we no longer need to fake confidence—we can claim it!

"Anyone who listens to my teaching and follows it is wise, like a person who builds a house on solid rock. Though the rain comes in torrents and the floodwaters rise and the winds beat against that house, it won't collapse because it is built on bedrock" (Matthew 7.24-25 NLT).

God, I want my life to be built on the Solid Rock of Jesus. I don't want my confidence to rise and fall depending on my own feelings, thoughts and actions. I want to walk out on the stages of life with a supernatural confidence that is rooted in You and not dependent on me. Show me how to accept grace. I know that Jesus died to give me His perfection through grace, and I will have the faith to claim it today. I no longer want to fake confidence. Instead, let my smile be genuine and based on a truth outside of myself. Teach me to walk in grace, so I can be a light to the world. I pray this in Jesus' name, amen.

Questions

- Have you ever had to fake a confident smile?
- Are you able to walk in grace?
- How can grace revolutionize your life?

Walk on stage with confident grace!

DAY 37: LEG CRAMP

Doing bodybuilding poses can be tiring. When making a pose, I'm actually forcing my muscles to do a static contraction. A static contraction is when you contract the muscle without moving it—or only moving it very little. For example, when I do a double bicep pose, I'm tensing every muscle in my body, especially the biceps, but I'm not pushing or pulling any resistance. This may seem easy, but it's actually a great workout. When I'm done practicing my bodybuilding poses, my heart is pounding and my muscles are worn out.

Toward the final days of my bodybuilding competition preparations, I was practicing my poses constantly. I could feel the tension in my muscles, and I noticed that my right calf muscle was on the verge of cramping. I got a massage a few days before my competition, and the therapist could feel the knots in my calf. She did her best to rub out the tension, but it was still very tight. During the prejudging, my calf finally cramped while I was on stage. Thankfully, I was doing a rear double bicep pose (my back was to the audience), so the judges did not see the shot of pain that went across my face. I recovered quickly and finished my routine. Although having a cramp on stage seemed like the worst thing that could happen, God allowed it to happen at just the right moment on stage.

Sometimes, God allows what we believe to be the worst thing imaginable to happen. We do everything to prevent it from happening, but no matter our efforts, the inevitable occurs. But what we don't realize is that God can line up all the elements in the situation, so that when the dreaded hardship occurs, it isn't so bad. It's almost like God is saying, "I'm going to allow this hardship, but It won't be as bad as you imagine it." Many times the fear of something is actually worse than the thing itself. Instead of fearing, we must choose to have faith. The world isn't fair and horrible and painful situations arise, but God will never leave us nor forsake us. And with God on our sides, we can endure anything.

"Praise be to the God and Father of our Lord Jesus Christ, the Father of compassion and the God of all comfort, who comforts us in all our troubles, so that we can comfort those in any trouble with the comfort we ourselves receive from God" (2 Corinthians 1.3-4 NIV).

God, I don't want to fear. Instead, fill me up with faith grounded in Your goodness and grace. I understand that sometimes bad things happen, but I trust that You will walk through dark times with me. I know that even in the bleakest situations, You can give me comfort and hope. Help me to find rest in Your reassurance. Forgive me if I've fretted over things instead of simply trusting in You and Your plan. I no longer want to worry about what can happen. I would rather take each day as it comes because I know that You give me what I need each day to stand firm in You. I pray this in Jesus' name, amen.

Questions

- Have you ever fretted over something bad that could happen?
- When the worst thing happened, how did God comfort you?
- Are you able to give your worries to God today?

Choose faith instead of fear!

DAY 38: FOUR SWORDS

My personal trainer worked very hard training me for nine months. Much of her thoughts, energy and time were concentrated on me and my bodybuilding competition. She helped me train my body, create a diet plan and learn my bodybuilding poses, and she also encouraged and motivated me. She felt the pressure for me to do well. There is much to bodybuilding competitions that can't be predicted, but each competitor can be as prepared as possible. My trainer was determined to make sure that I was ready. By the time I made it to my competition, I felt good about where I was physically and mentally. I had put all of my effort on the line, and my trainer was right there with me to guide and support me.

One of the best moments of the competition was watching my trainer carry my four trophies, which happened to be swords. The size of the swords were determined by the win. I had one small sword, which was for third place in the figure division. I had two medium swords, which were for second place in the novice physique division and the overall master's physique division. And I had one long sword, which was for first place in master's physique division for tall competitors. Seeing my trainer after nine months of hard work hold those swords in her arms was a priceless moment. I knew in my heart that those trophies were both of our wins. Yes, they hang on my wall, but I share them with her.

Most wins in our lives are not won alone. There are almost always people around us who encourage us and pour into us. These people are victory helpers and shapers. They may not get the trophy, but I believe that they receive eternal awards for their hard work. All of us will be on both sides of the victory: sometimes we will be the one winning the trophy and other times we will be the one carrying the trophy for others. We all have the ability to be victory helpers and shapers if we listen and follow the movement of the Holy Spirit. God wants His children to bless each other because He knows that we will find our true purpose when we serve those around us.

"For even the Son of Man did not come to be served, but to serve, and to give his life as a ransom for many" (Mark 10.45 NIV).

God, I want to be used by You to serve a greater purpose on earth. I know that You love Your people, and You want to see them blessed and victorious. Help me to be a part of those blessings and victories—not just my own but of those who are in my reach. I want to be a victory helper and shaper. I would be honored to be used. It doesn't matter if the trophy has my name on it or not. I simply want to be a part of something bigger than myself. I know that You have given me gifts and abilities that can fill a need and serve a purpose. Show me where I am needed today. I pray this in Jesus' name, amen.

Questions

- How has God used you to be a victory helper and shaper?
- Have you ever achieved a victory that was not your own?
- Can you thank the people who have helped you?

Be a victory helper and shaper!

DAY 39: HEALTHY HOME

I could have never competed in a bodybuilding competition without my family's support. I am a firm believer that if my family life and marriage are not healthy, I have no business going off and doing things that will add extra pressure to my home. Competing in a bodybuilding competition takes time, money, effort and energy, and I must always take care that my home life is healthy and vibrant first. The Ministry of the Home is my first priority, and I take my position as wife and mom very seriously. However, if I have poured into my family and my relationship with my husband, adding the pressure of a bodybuilding competition can be a healthy growth experience for all of us.

My entire family walked through the bodybuilding preparation and competition with me. They were so supportive and even enjoyed watching me on stage. My 7-year old daughter was so impressed with my first-place win that she couldn't wait to carefully hold the encased sword. My 10-year old son learned that all my days of sacrifice culminated into a single awesome moment that was worth the effort. It is one thing to watch Mommy work hard in the gym, but to watch her shine on stage gave him an upfront example of how hard work pays off. My oldest son who is 12-years old got to see me step outside of my comfort zone and do something new. I trust that in the future he will be more likely to take on new challenges because he has watched his mom do it and succeed.

Finally, I know my husband enjoyed watching me compete. It's easy in a marriage to get complacent with each other and not strive for new victories, but taking on a new challenge can be a wonderful experience for both people. My husband and I believe that dating should continue in a healthy marriage—whether at home or out on the town. We've been married for almost 18 years, and we enjoy each other's company more than ever. He liked watching me do something new and pushing forward even when it was hard work. We have both learned to grow in the Lord together. As long as we keep our eyes on Christ and keep Him the center of our marriage and family, we will always have a healthy and vibrant home life.

"She dresses herself with strength and makes her arms strong" (Proverbs 31.17 ESV).

God, I am honored to serve my family. I know that the home is Your design, and You love when families are healthy and strong. I know that Satan hates families because You created them, and he wants to do nothing but destroy our family and home life. But I will protect my family, marriage and home above all else. Only when I know that my family is healthy and vibrant will I take on the new challenges that You have given me. Please bless all of my adventures, and make me open to the fresh possibilities that You place before me. Lord, clothe me in strength and make my arms strong, so I can cultivate a healthy home, marriage and family life. I pray this in Jesus' name, amen.

Questions

- How is the health of your marriage and family?
- Is there an outside influence that is damaging your home?
- What adventure can you take your family on today?

Create a healthy, vibrant home life!

DAY 40: TAKING A BREAK

Bodybuilding takes a lot of effort, time and resources. After I finished my second competition, I came to a point where I would have to move forward growing muscle, getting leaner and competing more or I would have to take a break. Although I love being committed to a sport, I needed to ask myself what I wanted for my life. Did I want to be a professional bodybuilder or a professional writer? The answer was simple for me. My heart's desire and God's calling on my life has always been writing. I've written about the name of Jesus Christ for many years, and my purpose and design are rooted in sharing the Good News of the Cross. I am a Believer, wife, mother and writer. Lifting weights has been and will always be a hobby for me, but I'm not a bodybuilder by trade.

Of course, I still work out. I've been working out longer than I've been writing books, but it is something I do in my personal life, not professional life. I still want to lift heavy, break muscle and maintain the muscle that I've already achieved. But I have to make some changes in my lifestyle in order to put bodybuilding back where it belongs. First, I need to change my eating habits. I don't need as much protein since I'm not building muscle—only maintaining. Second, I must add a lot more cardio back into my schedule. I only lift a few days a week now, so the other days I run, use an exercise machine or work out to a video. Third, I don't have to drink so much water. Since I'm not breaking as much muscle, I don't need a gallon and a half of water every day to flush out the waste material.

Three simple changes helped me to change the course of my life. Many times the best changes we make are small. If we are feeling frustrated with our lifestyle or something feels off-kilter, doing something drastic—like moving, quitting a job, getting a divorce, or even cutting our hair—may not be the answer. A tire on a car can be off only a hundredth of a degree and cause a lot of wear and tear to the car, which puts the car under massive strain. Sometimes only a slight correction will make the car run smoothly again. When God is trying to move the direction of our lives, we can seek His divine positioning. Usually, He'll only tell us to make a few adjustments. We may be disappointed at first, but small adjustments to our daily life can make a huge impact overall. We will notice our lives run more smoothly and we are not wearing out so quickly.

"Jesus replied, 'But even more blessed are all who hear the word of God and put it into practice'" (Luke 11.28 NLT).

Father, show me where my life is out of alignment. I know that some days are more difficult than others, but I want to be aggressive about keeping the peace and joy in my every day. I feel that something is off-kilter. I know my life could be running more smoothly. Please pinpoint my problem areas and help me to make the correct adjustments to my actions. I can make a few adjustments and feel a true difference in my lifestyle. I want to first of all obey your basic commandments in the Bible, but I also want to obey the leading of the Holy Spirit all day. I trust that You will gently lead me into Your best and Your rest. I pray this in Jesus' name, amen.

Questions

- Is there something off-kilter in your life?
- What minor life adjustments can you make?
- Are there any behaviors in your life that need to be changed?

The best changes are small changes!

OTHER TITLES BY ALISA

Fiction

Eve of Awakening

Bear into Redemption

Nonfiction

Following God into the Cage

Fearlessly Fit

Imperfect Vessels

Broken Alabaster Jars

Gathering Empty Pitchers

Journey the Bible: Old Testament

Journey the Bible: New Testament

Our 6 His 7: Transformed by Sabbath Rest!

Made in the USA
Charleston, SC
16 February 2017